Pacific University
Harvey W. Scott Memorial Library

The William H. Studdiford '49
Endowed Collection in Theater

Photo by John Peter Weiss

Debra Mooney and George Grizzard in a scene from the Old
Globe Theatre (San Diego) production of "Another Antigone."
Set design by Steven Rubin.

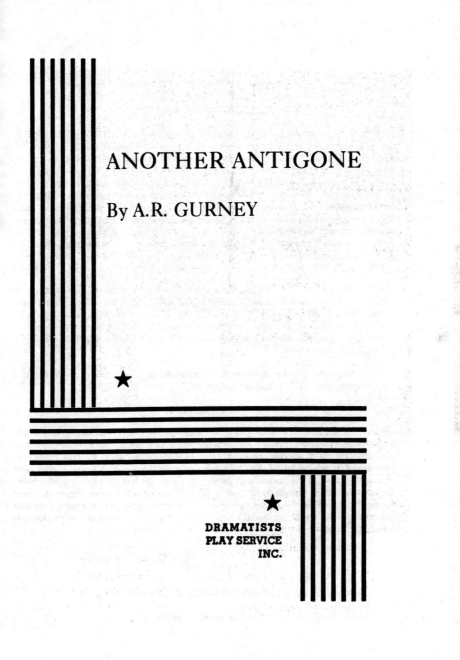

ANOTHER ANTIGONE

By A.R. GURNEY

DRAMATISTS
PLAY SERVICE
INC.

SOUND EFFECTS

The following is a list of sound effects referenced in this play:

Applause
Cheering crowd

ANOTHER ANTIGONE was first produced in March, 1987, at The Old Globe Theatre in San Diego, California, with the following cast:

HENRY .... George Grizzard

JUDY.................................. Marissa Chibas

DIANA .... Debra Mooney

DAVE................................... Steven Flynn

It was directed by John Tillinger, designed by Steven Rubin, lit by Kent Dorsey. The stage manager was Dianne De Vita.

The play opened at Playwrights Horizons in New York City in January, 1988. The cast, director, and designers remained the same. The stage manager, in this case, was Neal Ann Stephens.

To John Tillinger

CAST OF CHARACTERS

HENRY HARPER . . . . Professor of Classics

JUDY MILLER. . . . . a student

DIANA EBERHART . . . . Dean of Humane Studies

DAVID APPLETON . . . . a student

The play takes place in a university in Boston during the latter half of the spring term.

It is designed, as Sophocles' *Antigone* was, to be performed without an intermission. If one is deemed essential, however, it should occur after the third line on page 36.

The general effect of the set should evoke the Greek Revival architecture of a typical New England college. There should be columns and steps and benches. Somewhere in the center there should be a slightly abstracted desk and two chairs, indicating both Henry's and Diana's office. Near it is a bookcase, a filing cabinet, on which is an old hotplate, a possibly tin coffee pot, and a couple of cracked mugs. The general effect should be multi-scenic, fluid and shifting, indoors and out, and vaguely Greek.

ANOTHER ANTIGONE

AT RISE: Henry sits at his desk, perusing a typewritten paper. Judy sits in the other chair. She watches intently. He is middle-aged and conservatively dressed. She, in her early twenties, is casually dressed in whatever students are currently wearing.

HENRY. *(Finally, putting the document down neatly on the desk between them.)* Another Antigone.

JUDY. Did someone else write one?

HENRY. Sophocles wrote one.

JUDY. No, I mean someone in *class.*

HENRY. Aeschylus wrote one, which is lost. Euripides we *think* wrote one. Seneca tried to write one. Voltaire tried not to. Jean Anouilh wrote a rather peculiar one in 1944, during the Nazi occupation of Paris.

JUDY. But I'm the only one in *class* who wrote one.

HENRY. *(Weak smile.)* That's right. *(Pause.)* This year.

JUDY. You mean, other students wrote them in other years?

HENRY. Oh yes.

JUDY. Really?

HENRY. Of course. *(Henry goes to the filing cabinet. He pulls out a drawer.)* Let's see ... *Antigone* ... *Antigone* ... *(He thumbs through a file of old folders and records.)* Here we are. *Antigone. (He takes out a particular folder.)* Now. I have a record of one in 1955, written during the McCarthy hearings. And another, by a student who I recall was black, about the Civil Rights movement in 1963. And of course there were two, no, three, which cropped up during the Vietnam war.

JUDY. Did anyone ever deal with the Nuclear Arms Race before?

HENRY. No. As far as I know, you are the first to apply the Antigone myth to that particular topic.

JUDY. The story really turned me on.

HENRY. I'm glad it did. It is one of the great works of Western literature. Antigone herself is the classic rebel, the ancestor to such figures as Saint Joan or Martin Luther.

JUDY. Oh yes. I see that.

HENRY. And Creon is the ultimate image of uncompromising political authority.

JUDY. I got that, too.

HENRY. Their clash is inevitable and tragic.

JUDY. I understand. *(Indicating her manuscript.)* I tried to make them like Jane Fonda and Ronald Reagan.

HENRY. I know what you tried to do, Miss ... uh ... Miss ... *(He glances at her title page.)* Miller. I read all ... *(He glances at the last page.)* twelve pages of it, in preparation for this conference. *(He slides the script across the desk to her. She takes it, looks at the title page, flips through it, looks at the last page, then looks at him.)*

JUDY. You didn't mark it.

HENRY. I most certainly did. I underlined several run-on sentences, and I circled a rather startling number of misspelled words.

JUDY. No, I mean you didn't *grade* it.

HENRY. No I didn't.

JUDY. Why not?

HENRY. Because this course is about Greek tragedy, and your paper isn't.

JUDY. Did you grade those other *Antigone's?*

HENRY. I most certainly did not. I simply keep a record of them on file, the way the Pope keeps a file on various heresies.

JUDY. Well mine isn't a heresy!

HENRY. It is, to me.

JUDY. Don't you believe in nuclear disarmament?

HENRY. Of course I do. I think the arms race is madness.

JUDY. Then don't you think these things should be said?

HENRY. Absolutely. And I believe I said them, back in February, when I was discussing the political background of Greek

6

drama. Then, if you'll remember, I compared Athens and Sparta, and pointed out rather frightening analogies to the United States and the Soviet Union.

JUDY. I had mono in February.

HENRY. Mono?

JUDY. Nucleosis. I kept falling asleep at the Film Festival, even during *Psycho*.

HENRY. I'm sorry to hear that. You must get the notes, then, from a fellow student. You might need them when you write your term paper.

JUDY. But this *is* my term paper.

HENRY. It's not on an assigned topic.

JUDY. It's on *Antigone*.

HENRY. But it's not on Sophocles.

JUDY. But I spent two weeks working on it.

HENRY. Sophocles spent two years.

JUDY. But I'm taking other courses!

HENRY. And Sophocles didn't — I grant you.

JUDY. Yes, but...

HENRY. Miss Miller: At the beginning of the semester, I handed out a list of assigned topics. I stated specifically that any departures from these topics should be cleared through me. Now suddenly, long before the term is over, I discover this odd effort, stuffed under my door, with no previous permission whatsoever.

JUDY. I had to try it first. To see if it worked.

HENRY. Well, you did. And it didn't.

JUDY. So what do I do?

HENRY. You read the texts carefully. You attend class religiously. And in the middle of May, you hand in a fifteen-page, coherently organized, typewritten paper, with adequate margins and appropriate footnotes, on the main issues of this course.

JUDY. Couldn't you give me partial credit? For the idea?

HENRY. Miss Miller, how can I? It's misguided. It's wrong. You have taken one of the world's great plays, and reduced it to a juvenile polemic on current events.

JUDY. Juvenile?

HENRY. I'm sorry.

JUDY. Of course that's your opinion.

HENRY. I'm afraid my opinion is the one that counts.

JUDY. But what if I put it on?

HENRY. On?

JUDY. In front of the class — just reading it out loud.

HENRY. Miss Miller: we have only so much time before the end of the term. We have yet to absorb the very difficult concept of Greek tragedy. I doubt if there's time in class to play show-and-tell.

JUDY. Then I'll do it somewhere else.

HENRY. I'd spend my time on a paper.

JUDY. I'll do my play instead. You could come and see.

HENRY. I'm afraid I'd see a great gap in your education, Miss Miller. As well as in my list of grades.

JUDY. You mean I'd fail?

HENRY. You'd receive an incomplete.

JUDY. Which means, since I'm a senior, that I'd fail. I wouldn't graduate, Professor Harper.

HENRY. Which means you'd better not spend these last valuable days of your academic life on amateur theatrics. *(He gets up, begins organizing his books and notes.)* And now I have to teach a class. And I strongly suspect you have to go to one. *(Judy gets up, too.)*

JUDY. Professor Harper, I don't want to sound conceited or any-thing, but you should know that after I graduate, I've been accep-ted for a special training program in investment banking at Morgan Guaranty Trust in New York City.

HENRY. My congratulations.

JUDY. Well, in my interview, they were particularly impressed by my leadership qualities, my creativity, and my personal sense of commitment. They wrote me that in a letter, Professor Harper.

HENRY. Congratulations again.

JUDY. I also heard, from someone who works there, that I'm only the second Jewish woman to be brought into that program at that level since its inception.

HENRY. I am virtually overwhelmed.

8

JUDY. Yes, well, I believe in my abilities, Professor Harper. I plan to apply them. I'm going to put this play *on*. I wrote it, and I like it, and I'm committed to what it says. And if it's no good now, I'll work to make it better. And I'll bet, by the end of the term, you'll be able to give me a straight A.

HENRY. *(Turning, as if at the door.)* Miss Miller: After such a magnificent display of American optimism and industry, I'm tempted to give you a straight A right now.

JUDY. Thank you.

HENRY. And I believe I would if this were a course on comedy. But alas, it is not. It's a course on tragedy. And you have just demonstrated that you have no conception of tragedy at all! *(He goes off, with his books and notes. Judy looks at him, and looks at her paper. She goes off, reading it aloud.)*

JUDY.

People of this land, we suffer under a yoke.

(She begins to realize a new pertinence.)

A tyrant rules our city, and unjust laws
Now squelch all forms of perfectly plausible protest ...

(She goes off. As she goes off, Diana comes on to address the audience. She is a harassed, nervous, middle-aged woman, dressed efficiently. She speaks to the audience as if it were a group of concerned students. She might speak from note cards.)

DIANA. Good morning ... I spoke to you as freshmen. I speak to you now as seniors and what we hope will be very generous alumni ... The topic of today's meeting is "Preparing for the Future." I'll be brief, since I know all of you are waiting to hear from the Placement people about the world beyond these walls. I do want to make a quick comment on our curriculum, however. A number of you have recently complained about the traditional courses which are still required. Why, you ask, with tuitions so high and the search for jobs so increasingly competitive, are you forced to take such impractical courses? You may be sure, by the way, that the recruiting offices at I.B.M. and General Electric are asking the same question: Why must you take these things? After all, they are concerned only with some book, some poem, some old play. "Only some work," as my special favorite Jane Austen once said, "in which the best powers of the mind are displayed, in the best chosen language." Well, there you are. They're the best. And we need no reason beyond that to justify, for example, Professor Harper's course on Greek tragedy. It deals with the best. It exists. It is there. And will remain there, among several other valuable requirements, for what we hope is a very long time. *(She glances offstage.)* And now, Alice Zimmerman, from Placement, will talk to you about ... *(She glances at her note card.)* "The Job Market Jungle versus the Graduate School Grind." Those of you who are tardy may now be seated. *(The late members of the audience may be seated here.)* Have a good morning. *(She goes off as Dave comes on from another direction. He reads aloud from a typewritten script.)*

DAVE.
"No, Antigone, no. Please reconsider.
Do not take on this dangerous enterprise.
The risks are too great, the payoff insignificant."
(Judy comes on, as if down the steps of the library, carrying a stack of books.)

JUDY. *(Breathlessly.)* Look what I got. *(Reads off the titles.)* The Nuclear Insanity ... A World Beyond War ... Our Debt to the Future ... I'm going to put all this in.

DAVE. You're racking up a lot of time on this thing.

JUDY. Well I want to make it good. Did you read the first scene?

DAVE. *(Reciting by heart.)*
"No, Antigone, no. Please reconsider."

JUDY. What do you think? *(Pause.)*

DAVE. You're in blank verse.

JUDY. I know that.

DAVE.
Every line.
(Accentuates it.)
"Do *not* take *on* this *dang'*rous *enterprise*."

JUDY. I know.

DAVE. How come?

10

JUDY. *(Accenting it.)* I *just* got *in*to *it* and *cou*ldn't *stop.*

DAVE. *(Dramatically, as if it were Shakespeare.)*
"The risks are too great, the payoff insignificant."

JUDY. Want to do this?

DAVE. Me?

JUDY. Want to?

DAVE. *(Looking at script.)* This is a woman's part. This is her sister talking here.

JUDY. I've changed it. I've made it her lover.

DAVE. Get someone from Drama.

JUDY. I already did. Drama people are doing all the other roles. Please, Dave. Do it.

DAVE. *(Melodramatically.)*
"No, Antigone, no. Please reconsider."
(Pause.) I better not, Judy.

JUDY. I need company.

DAVE. No thanks.

JUDY. I thought you liked Greek stuff.

DAVE. I do.

JUDY. You even talked me into taking the course.

DAVE. I know, I know.

JUDY. You're always borrowing the books ...

DAVE. Yeah, but I don't have time for anything anymore. I've got a double lab in my major this term. And a brutal schedule in track every weekend. And, as you know, I'm not doing too well in either.

JUDY. You're doing fine. You're just a slow starter. *(Slyly.)* Which is part of your charm.

DAVE. All I know is, you get straight A's, you've got a great job waiting for you on the outside, you can afford to fool around with drama. Me? I've only had one interview so far, and I blew it.

JUDY. You didn't *blow* it, Dave. You just overslept.

DAVE. Yeah well, how can we live together next year if I can't nail down a job in New York? I've got to get my grades up, Jude.

JUDY. All right, Dave. That's cool. I'll look for someone else. *(She takes her own copy of her script out of her backpack, looks at it, looks at him.)* Would you at least read it with me?

DAVE. Sure.

JUDY. From the top?

DAVE. Sure. Why not? *(Reading.)*
"Hello, Antigone. And what brings you here,
Worried and out of sorts on this spring morning?
You look like you've got something on —
(Pause.)
— your mind."

JUDY. *(Reading.)*
"My friend Lysander — "

DAVE. *(Looking at his script.)* Lysander? I have "Beloved sister."

JUDY. That's what I changed. I changed it to Lysander.

DAVE. Lysander? That's Shakespeare. It's from *Midsummer Night's Dream.*

JUDY. It's also Greek. I looked it up.

DAVE. But it primarily —

JUDY. *(Reads, with feeling.)*
"My friend Lysander, will you join with me
In picketing and protesting the bomb
At several local military bases
Where nuclear arms are stored? And would you be willing,
O my loyal Lysander — "

DAVE. Lysander. Sounds like a disinfectant.

JUDY. *(Insistently.)*
"Would you be willing, O my loyal Lysander
Even to chain yourself to a chain-link fence
Or lie down in the road in front of a gate
And so prevent all types of vehicular access?"

DAVE. I do.

JUDY.
"And if the state police or National Guard,
Accompanied by snarling German shepherds,
Attempted to dislodge us from our task,
Would you be willing, my lover and my friend ...

12

To go to jail with me, and there remain
At least till our parents post appropriate bail.
(Pause.)
DAVE. Who'll you get for Lysander if I don't do it?
JUDY. Oh probably that blond fraternity type who lifts weights
and played the lead in *Fool for Love.*
DAVE. Mark Shapiro? *(Judy nods.)* I'll do Lysander.
JUDY. Now don't if you don't want to.
DAVE. So I get another C in another course.
JUDY. Now think positively, Dave.
DAVE. So I mess up another interview.
JUDY. *(Handing him her script.)* I'll buy you a new alarm clock.
Read from here.
DAVE. *(Looking at it.)* This is all new.
JUDY. I rewrote it last night. With you in mind.
DAVE. You knew I'd do it.
JUDY. I hoped you would. *(Henry reenters his office, settles into a
chair to read a book.)*
DAVE. *(Kissing her.)*
"Antigone ...
(Then reading.)
Much as I've loved you, even since freshman year,
And lived with you since the second semester of sophomore,
Built you a loft for our bed in off-campus housing,
Prepared your pasta, shared your stereo,
Still I have fears about what you've just proposed.
The risks are too great, the payoff insignificant."
JUDY. What do you think?
DAVE. I love it.
JUDY. You do?
DAVE. I love you.
JUDY. *(Taking the script back.)* I don't like it.
DAVE. What's the matter?
JUDY. It sounds wrong. I'm going to rewrite it.
DAVE. Again?
JUDY. *(Gathering up her books and bag.)* I'll make it better.

13

DAVE. What if you cut Lysander?

JUDY. Why? You're good. I'm going to build up his part.

DAVE. *(Following her.)*

"No, Antigone, no. Please reconsider."

(They go off as Diana appears in the doorway to Henry's office.)

DIANA. Henry?

HENRY. Yes? Come in. *(He sees her and jumps to his feet.)* Ah. Our Dean. Empress of all Humanities, including Remedial Reading. *(He gives her an elaborately courtly salute and bow.)*

DIANA. Knock if off, Henry.

HENRY. You look particularly lovely today, Diana. What is it? New hairdo? New blouse? New something.

DIANA. It's the same old me, Henry.

HENRY. No, no. There's something different. Maybe it's your eyes. They blaze like beacons 'cross The Hellespont.

DIANA. And it's the same old you, Henry. You've been saying things like that for twenty years.

HENRY. And meaning them, Diana.

DIANA. I used to think you meant them. Now I know different.

HENRY. Dear lady ...

DIANA. Now I know that you just say these things by rote, Henry. You say them to the librarian in the reserve book room, and you say them to the Xerox woman, and you say them to the cashier in the cafeteria. You say them to keep us all at a distance, so you won't have to say anything else. If any of us *did* have a new blouse, you wouldn't notice it at all.

HENRY. Now, Diana ...

DIANA. Let's change the channel, shall we, Henry? Something's come up.

HENRY. What dark words seek to escape through the gate of thy teeth?

DIANA. Judy Miller.

HENRY. Judy ... ?

DIANA. Miller. *(Pause.)*

HENRY. Ah. Miss Miller. *(French accent.)* L'affaire Antigone.

DIANA. You know that's why I'm here, Henry.

HENRY. I swear I didn't. I have a number of students, a number of courses.

DIANA. You teach two courses, Henry. And you have relatively few students in each. Now let's focus, please, on the issue.

HENRY. Administration has made you cruel as Clytemnestra.

DIANA. Henry, *please. (Pause.)*

HENRY. All right. Judy Miller.

DIANA. I understand —

HENRY. Would you like some coffee? *(He crosses to pour her some.)*

DIANA. Yes, please — I understand she brought in a re-written version.

HENRY. She brought in *two* rewritten versions.

DIANA. Well she brought one to me, as well.

HENRY. The first? Or the second?

DIANA. A third.

HENRY. I said I wouldn't read that one.

DIANA. It's not bad, Henry. It's longer, it's getting better. It's now at least a play.

HENRY. It's hopeless.

DIANA. Give her a B for effort.

HENRY. A *B?* I won't give her any grade at all.

DIANA. A student takes our course, becomes inspired by an old play, writes a modern version ...

HENRY. And demonstrates thereby that she knows nothing about Sophocles, nothing about the Greeks, nothing about tragedy.

DIANA. Henry, she tried.

HENRY. And failed. A B? A B means good. A B means very good. I am not so far lost in the current inflation of grades as to litter the campus with disposable Bs.

DIANA. Oh, Henry ...

HENRY. I'm sorry. If I gave her a grade for that nonsense, Diana, it would make the whole course meaningless. *(Pause.)* It would make *me* meaningless. *(Pause. Diana lights a cigarette.)* Still smoking, I see.

15

DIANA. Sometimes.

HENRY. Don't.

DIANA. I smoke, Henry, when I find myself caught in the middle of something. Which seems to be the case a good deal lately with this job.

HENRY. Ah hah. Second thoughts from our Dean. You asked for that job, Diana. You agitated for it. All that chatter about the need for more women at the administrative level. Well, now you've sunk to that level and it's leveling you. Come back to the classroom where you belong.

DIANA. Sometimes I wish I could.

HENRY. *(Taking an ashtray out of a desk drawer, holding it out to her.)* At least put out that cigarette. Life is tragic enough without your contributing to it.

DIANA. Let me enjoy it, Henry.

HENRY. Your lungs or mine, Diana. *(He holds out the ashtray.)* Put it out.

DIANA. You win. *(She puts it out; he cleans out the ashtray, puts it away.)* Now let me win one.

HENRY. No.

DIANA. How about partial credit?

HENRY. No.

DIANA. She's a senior. She needs to graduate.

HENRY. I'm sorry. *(Pause.)*

DIANA. She's putting it on, you know.

HENRY. The play?

DIANA. She's putting it on.

HENRY. Reading it? In some dining hall?

DIANA. Staging it. She asked my permission to use Spingler Auditorium.

HENRY. You said No.

DIANA. I said Yes.

HENRY. You gave her permission?

DIANA. Of course I gave it to her. I had to give it to her. *(Pause.)* I wanted to give it to her.

HENRY. Traitor. Or is it, Traitress?

16

DIANA. Well, I'm sorry, Henry. But there seems to be a lot of interest cropping up for this thing. Several of the student anti-nuclear groups want to sponsor it. Bill Silverstein is writing some incidental music on the Moog Synthesizer. And someone over in Art has agreed to do simple neo-classic scenery. They plan to present it on the Friday night before graduation. For parents. And alumni. And friends.

HENRY. Poor Sophocles ...

DIANA. Oh now.

HENRY. Set to the tune of a Moog Synthesizer.

DIANA. Yes well, it should create quite a stir.

HENRY. Quite a stir! That's it, exactly, Diana! Quite a stir! It will stir up a lot of cheap liberal guilt and a lot of fake liberal piety and a lot of easy liberal anger at the poor Creons of this world who are really working on this nuclear thing, and frantically trying to keep the world from blowing itself up!

DIANA. Oh, Henry ...

HENRY. Do you know what tragedy is, Diana?

DIANA. I think I do, yes.

HENRY. I don't think you do, Diana. I don't think anyone in this happy-ending country really does. Tragedy means the universe is unjust and unfair, Diana. It means we are hedged about by darkness, doom, and death. It means the good, the just, and well-intentioned don't always *win*, Diana. That's what tragedy means. And if we can learn that, if I can teach that, if I can give these bright, beady-eyed students at least a glimmer of that, then perhaps someday we will be able to join hands with our enemies across the water, or our neighbors down below, or the outcasts in our own back*yard*, and create a common community against this darkness. That's what I believe, Diana. And that's what Sophocles believed in 443 B.C. when he wrote *Antigone*. That's what Shakespeare believed when he wrote *King Lear*. Tragedy keeps us honest, keeps us real, keeps us human. All great nations should have a tragic vision, Diana, and we have none. And that is why I cannot endorse what this woman, no, this *girl*, is doing when she puts on her strident little travesty for the passing parade in Spingler Auditorium on

17

graduation weekend. That is not tragedy, Diana. That is just trouble-making. And I cannot give her credit for it. *(Pause.)*

DIANA. May I have the ashtray back, please?

HENRY. No.

DIANA. I want it *back*, Henry. I don't want to tap ashes all over your floor.

HENRY. *(Handing it to her.)* Here. *(Gets up.)* I'll open the door.

DIANA. I'd leave the door closed, Henry. Open the window if you want. This is private. *(She smokes.)*

HENRY. *(Not opening anything.)* Private?

DIANA. Have you given any thoughts to your low enrollments, Henry?

HENRY. Thought? Of course I've given thought. In a world of television and Punk Rock, it's a little difficult to maintain —

DIANA. The Provost thinks there might be another reason, Henry.

HENRY. The Provost?

DIANA. He brought it up last fall, when he saw the registration figures.

HENRY. And what does the Provost think?

DIANA. Apparently... over the years... there've been complaints about you, Henry.

HENRY. Oh I'm sure. That I take attendance. That I take off for misspellings. That I actually *call* on people in class.

DIANA. No, it's something else, Henry. Some students ... over the years ... have complained that you're ... biased.

HENRY. Biased?

DIANA. Prejudiced.

HENRY. *Pre*judiced?

DIANA. Anti-Semitic, Henry. *(Pause.)*

HENRY. Say that again.

DIANA. There's been a pattern of complaints.

HENRY. But on what *grounds?*

DIANA. Apparently the administration thinks you make certain remarks in the classroom. Which students pass on. And cause

18

others to stay away. *(Pause.)*

HENRY. This is ridiculous.

DIANA. I agree.

HENRY. And outrageous.

DIANA. I think so, too.

HENRY. It's slander! I'm going to see the Provost right now!

DIANA. Hold on, Henry!

HENRY. I mean this is unconscionable. It's like the time five years ago when poor Bob Klein was accused of some late night unpleasantness in the lab by that little temptress in a T-shirt. He had to resign.

DIANA. He resigned because he was *guilty,* Henry.

HENRY. Well I'm not guilty of anti-Semitism. Or do you think I am?

DIANA. I think you ... make remarks, Henry.

HENRY. Remarks?

DIANA. For example, in the curriculum meeting last fall ...

HENRY. What did I say?

DIANA. You told that joke.

HENRY. It was a good joke. I got that joke from Jack Nathanson.

DIANA. Well no one laughed when *you* told it, Henry. And no one laughed when you delivered that diatribe against Israel last week at lunch.

HENRY. That wasn't supposed to be funny.

DIANA. Well it certainly wasn't.

HENRY. I mean, when you think how we let one small country so totally dominate our foreign policy ...

DIANA. Henry!

HENRY. Well I mean it's insane! It's suicidal! Pericles warned us about it in 426 B.C.: "Beware of entanglements in Asia Minor," he said.

DIANA. Henry, Dick Livingston was sitting right across the *table* when you said those things!

HENRY. Is Dick Jewish?

DIANA. *I'm* Jewish, Henry.

19

HENRY. *You're* Jewish?

DIANA. Half Jewish. My mother was an Austrian Jew.

HENRY. I didn't know that.

DIANA. Well I am. And Judy Miller is Jewish. *(Pause.)*

HENRY. Has she complained that I'm prejudiced?

DIANA. No. *She* hasn't ...

HENRY. But you still think I'm some raving neo-Nazi who is pumping anti-Semitic propaganda into his courses three times a week?

DIANA. *(Quietly.)* No. I think you're a passionate teacher and scholar, whose lectures are loaded with extravagant analogies which are occasionally misinterpreted by sensitive Jewish students.

HENRY. And the Provost?

DIANA. The Provost thinks it's an issue which should never even arise. Seeing as how we're in the middle of a major fund drive. And more and more, it seems to be Jewish generosity that's keeping us all afloat.

HENRY. *(Thinking.)* I do the Auerbach thing at the beginning of the term.

DIANA. The Auerbach thing?

HENRY. A great scholar. Jewish, Diana. And superb! He sees two fundamental themes in Western culture. The Greek and the Hebraic. Odysseus versus Abraham. Public honor versus private conscience.

DIANA. Well maybe that starts you off on the wrong foot.

HENRY. No, no. It works marvelously. I carry it further. I build to the basic contrast between Athens and Jerusalem.

DIANA. Well maybe those generalizations could be taken the wrong way.

HENRY. Do you think so?

DIANA. Henry: This is a free country. And academic life is even more so. You may write four-letter words all over the blackboard. You may denounce the government, blaspheme God, take off your clothes ...

HENRY. Good Heavens, Diana ...

DIANA. You may do all of these things in here, and most of them

20

out there. But there is one thing, here and there, you may not do. You may *not* be insensitive about the Jews. That is taboo. The twentieth century is still with us, Henry. We live in the shadow of the Holocaust. Remember that, please. And be warned. *(Pause.)*

HENRY. I hear you, Diana.

DIANA. Thank you.

HENRY. I'll stay simply with the Greeks. I'll lash myself to the mast, and avoid the Bible. I'll even avoid the Book of Job.

DIANA. Thank you, Henry.

HENRY. I must say, Diana, I've never really understood the Old Testament anyway. All that brooding, internal self-laceration. And the sense of a special contract with God. The sense of being chosen. The sense of sure salvation somewhere on down the line. Have you ever felt that? I haven't. But the Jews must feel it. Even after Auschwitz, they feel it. Perhaps because of Auschwitz, they feel it all the more. I suppose that's why they put so much stock in their children. They spoil them, you know. Their children are generally spoiled. They bring them to dinner parties. They teach them to feel — what is that word? — "entitled." Perhaps that's why this girl, excuse me, this woman, this Miss Miller, feels so strongly she deserves special treatment.

DIANA. Henry.

HENRY. My children don't feel that way. I taught my children to tow the mark. To take their turn. To submit to authority. Of course, that hasn't worked out so well either. I mean, I don't hear from my children much anymore. The Jews hear from their children. Their children telephone them all the time. *(Turns to her.)* I'm painting myself into a corner, aren't I?

DIANA. Yes you are, Henry.

HENRY. Yes. Well. You're right. All this could be ... misinterpreted. I'll try to be more careful.

DIANA. Yes, I would, Henry. Because the Provost is talking about cutting back.

HENRY. Cutting back?

DIANA. On courses that are — undersubscribed.

21

HENRY. My course on tragedy is required!

DIANA. Your course is on a *list* of *several* required courses. And the Provost can take it off that list any time.

HENRY. What? Tear from the Tree of Knowledge one of the last golden apples that still remain? A course that survived the ghastly chaos of the sixties? A course that —

DIANA. Henry, he can do it.

HENRY. I'll be more careful ... "Whom the Gods would destroy, they first drive mad."

DIANA. Yes, well, and it might be a good idea, Henry — just to avoid any misunderstanding — to give Judy Miller a grade for what she's done. *(Pause.)*

HENRY. You *think* so?

DIANA. Yes I do. Otherwise you might come out of this whole thing looking very much like Creon in that damn play.

HENRY. This is not a tragedy by Sophocles, Diana. It is a comedy by Aristophanes, at best. I am not Creon, and that little Jewish princess is not Antigone, Princess of Thebes.

DIANA. Cool it, Henry!

HENRY. *(With great reluctance.)* I'll give her a D. For Determination.

DIANA. Henry ...

HENRY. *(Angrily.)* All right. A C, then. For Commitment.

DIANA. I don't think she'll accept a C.

HENRY. Won't *accept?*

DIANA. She feels she deserves a good grade.

HENRY. She'll get a good grade when she shows me some small awareness of what tragedy is. Lord knows she's shown me what it isn't. *(Judy comes out now. She sits on some steps or a bench D., takes a spiral notebook out of her backpack, and writes in it, concentratedly. Diana sighs and gets up.)*

DIANA. If I were you, Henry, I'd head for the hills of New Hampshire after your last class. I wouldn't want to be around when the grades go in and that play goes on and that girl doesn't graduate. Go up to your cottage, chop wood, disconnect the telephone.

HENRY. I don't like to go up there alone.

DIANA. Oh dear. Trouble again?

HENRY. Elsa's moved out. Again.

DIANA. She'll be back.

HENRY. I don't think so. She says now the children have gone, I'm impossible to live with.

DIANA. Now where did she get an idea like that? *(She goes out. Henry exits, after a moment, another way. The lights come up more fully on Judy, hard at her writing on the steps in the sun. Dave comes on carrying a paperback book.)*

DAVE. Hi.

JUDY. *(Looking up from her work.)* Hey, aren't you supposed to be in Chemistry?

DAVE. Missed it. Lost track of the time.

JUDY. But you flunked the last quiz.

DAVE. I got hung up reading one of your books.

JUDY. Which one?

DAVE. *(Showing her.)* Sophocles ... *Antigone.*

JUDY. Oh. *(Pause.)*

DAVE. It's good.

JUDY. It's fair.

DAVE. It's awesome.

JUDY. It's good.

DAVE. Maybe we should do that version.

JUDY. What about mine?

DAVE. Maybe you'd get your A if you did Sophocles.

JUDY. I've thought about that, Dave: In Sophocles, all she wants to do is bury one dead brother.

DAVE. True.

JUDY. In mine, she sees everyone in the *world* as her brother, and she's fighting to keep them all *alive.*

DAVE. O.K., Jude. *(He sits down beside her, takes out a banana.)* Want some?

JUDY. No thanks.

DAVE. *(As he eats.)* While I was reading, your dad called.

JUDY. Again?

DAVE. From the hospital. Between patients.

JUDY. What did he want?

DAVE. He wants you to graduate.

JUDY. I'll graduate.

DAVE. He wants to be sure.

JUDY. Did you tell him I'm appealing to the Grievance Committee? Did you say that the Dean herself is presenting my case?

DAVE. He said committees make him nervous.

JUDY. Well, parents make *me* nervous.

DAVE. He said he hasn't spent thirty years in the lower intestine just so his daughter could flunk college.

JUDY. Sounds familiar.

DAVE. He said write the paper. Get the degree. Argue with the professor after.

JUDY. That's my father.

DAVE. That's everyone's father.

JUDY. Actually, I got a letter from my mother today.

DAVE. Coordinated attack, huh.

JUDY. She wrote from her office. On her "Department of Mental Health" stationery. Saying I was just acting out my guilt for being so lucky in life.

DAVE. You are lucky.

JUDY. I know. and I know they've worked hard to keep it that way. Moving to Westport, so I could grow up in a "healthy suburban environment." Sending me to Andover, so I could frolic in preppy heaven. Europe last summer, so I could learn how to use a credit card. Hell, four years *here,* for God's sake. And now they're offering to pay a psychiatrist two hundred dollars a week so I can blame it all on them.

DAVE. You're kidding!

JUDY. My mother even enclosed a note from my grandmother saying that Jewish people should bend over backwards not to make waves.

DAVE. Got you surrounded, huh?

JUDY. Sure have.

DAVE. They all just want you to do well.

JUDY. I know that. I appreciate that.

DAVE. Look. Why not hedge your bets? Do the play *and* write the paper.

JUDY. I *can't,* Dave. I've tried and I can't. It all comes out fake and phony and not me.

DAVE. Then take the C. The Dean says Harper will give you that. Take it, and run.

JUDY. I can't do that either.

DAVE. Why *not?*

JUDY. I don't know, Dave. Here I am working with a bunch of really dedicated people ... trying to reach out to the local community ... on a subject which deals with the survival of the entire planet ... don't you think that's worth a tad more than a C, Dave?

DAVE. Sure it is.

JUDY. Then let me go for it.

DAVE. O.K. Let's rehearse. *(He tosses the banana peel into a trash can with a basketball leap.)*

JUDY. Thanks, Dave. *(She hugs him.)* Listen to this new stuff. *(She reads what she has just written.)*
"Lately I'm feeling very much alone.
Even you, Lysander, seem to be backing off,
Advising caution, counseling compromise."

DAVE. *(Reading over her shoulder.)*
"I just don't want to see you get in trouble.
Just think what they could do to you, Antigone:
They could throw you in jail, there to be beaten up
By roving gangs of angry lesbians.
Or worse:
They could banish you, and send you off
With no degree to grace your resume
To fritter away essential earning years
In waitressing or joining a typing pool."

JUDY. *(Reading.)*
"Still, my conscience tells me I am right.
And if I am to suffer — "
(She stops; looks at him.)

25

DAVE. What's the matter?

JUDY. Maybe I *am* just being a brat.

DAVE. No, no ...

JUDY. A spoiled little JAP, playing sixties-type games as a last gasp before facing up to the real world ...

DAVE. Naaa ...

JUDY. Maybe I should just take a massive all-nighter in the library, and grunt out one of those boring, studenty papers with a title like "Tragic Irony in Sophocles" or some such thing.

DAVE. Sounds good to me. Want me to help?

JUDY. You don't have time. *(Looking at her notebook; reading.)*
"And yet this stupid arms race still goes on.
Oh it appalls me! God, it makes me mad!
(She begins to gather steam.)
It's as if the United States and Soviet Russia
Were two small boys comparing penises
With the fate of the world dependent on the outcome!"

DAVE. *(Covering his crotch.)* Right on, Antigone!

JUDY. *(Cranking up.)*
"Oh men, men, men!
Why are you all — with only a few exceptions —
(A glance at Dave.)
So miserably hung up on competition?
The Air Force General, the Corporation Executive,
The College Professor tyrannizing his students ... "

DAVE. *(Looking over her shoulder.)* Hey! Where's that line? I don't see that.

JUDY. I'm improvising! I'm winging it!
"The College Professor tyrannizing his students,
It seems the entire world is under the thumb
Of self-important men. I fear, Lysander,
That one of these days, one of these little men
Will reach across his desk and push the button
Which will destroy us all!"

DAVE. Now that's pretty good.

JUDY. *(Gathering up her stuff.)* No it isn't. And you know it isn't.

But I'll make it better. *(She starts off.)*
DAVE. *(Starting after her.)* I'll give you a hand.
JUDY. You better make up that chemistry. There's no reason for you to flunk out, even if I do. *(She goes.)*
DAVE. *(Calling after her.)* But I really want to — *(He looks at the Sophocles still in his hand, gets an idea, concludes quietly.)* Help. *(He goes off the opposite way as Henry enters to teach his class. He carries an old, worn leather book, stuffed with scraps of paper. He might use half-lens reading glasses, so that he can peer out at the audience as necessary.)*
HENRY. It might be particularly appropriate at this point in the course to let Sophocles speak for himself. I will try to translate for you — directly from the Greek — portions of the great choral ode from the *Antigone*. I will attempt to make it speak as immediately as I can. And I hope, as you hear it, you will compare it to other local efforts on this subject that may have come to your attention in recent weeks. *(Opening his book, finding his place, translating with great feeling.)*
"There are many wondrous things in the world,
But nothing is more wondrous than Man."
(Looks up.) Deinos ... "wondrous" ... the other day I heard one of you use the word "awesome." All right. Let's try *awesome. (Returns to text.)*
"Nothing is more awesome than Man."
(Looks up; sighs.) Or yes. All right. Today: woman. The point is nothing is more awesome than the human being. Here I used to contrast this awesome view with the rather abject and quarrelsome vision of man emerging in the Old Testament. But I won't do that now. Rather, returning to the text ... *(He does.)* I will simply call your attention to the series of magnificent images on the taming of nature: ships, plows, fishnets, ox-yokes ... *(Looks up.)* Today planes, rockets, computers, laser beams ... *(Returns to text.)*
"which man has created through his uncanny technology."
(Looks up.) And then come our social inventions, those things we have invented to tame ourselves ... *(Translates.)* "language which leads to thought" ... "laws" ... "medicine" ... "religion" ... "cities"

27

... *(Looks up.)* There it is. The city. The *polis.* The human community. The result of all this creative activity. We'll come back to that. *(Translates.)*

"Man — or woman — is resourceful in everything, and proudly prepares for the future. *But ... "*

(Looks up.) There is a big But here ... *But ... (Translates.)*

"There is one thing he can't tame, can't control: and that is Death."

(Looks up.) All right now, death was terrifying — the Greeks loved life — but Sophocles goes on to mention something *worse* than death. *(Looks at text.)* and here comes the crack of the whip: *(Translates grimly.)*

"Yet if, for the sake of pride, he ...

(Looks up; is glad to use the feminine this time.) Or *she ... (Returns to text.)*

"Goes too far, then he becomes an exile ... "

(Looks up.) Which to the Greek was far, far worse than death. *(Translates.)*

"An exile without a country,

Lost and alone,

Homeless and outlawed forever."

You see? Sophocles joyfully celebrates the lawful human community, the Greek *polis,* but then threatens those who defy it with a death beyond death — exile, banishment, ostracism. *(Returns to the text.)*

"Lost and alone.

Homeless and outlawed forever."

(Looks up.) Last year, I compared these grim lines to the Hebrew's lamentations in the Psalms. This year, I will try to conjure up other images of profound alienation: *(He thinks.)* The haunted Orestes ... Napoleon dying his slow death on the desolate island of Saint Helena ... some lost astronaut severed forever from the good, green earth ... *(Returns to the text.)*

"Homeless and outlawed forever."

(Pause.) Those words were written over two thousand years ago. I have read and taught them countless times. I get shivers up and

down my spine every time I do. *(The bell rings. He closes his book.)* I think even Sophocles would commend my theatrical timing. For the next session, read *The Trojan Women* by Euripides. Feminists will appreciate his sympathetic portrayal of women. Pacifists will admire his bitter attack on war. Classicists, however, prefer to reach beyond such limited responses. Thank you, and good afternoon. *(He gathers his books as Dave approaches him.)*

DAVE. Professor Harper?

HENRY. *(Turning.)* Yes?

DAVE. I'm a friend of Judy's.

HENRY. Judy?

DAVE. Miss Miller.

HENRY. Ah.

DAVE. *(Holding out envelope.)* She asked me to give you this.

HENRY. "Has she sent poison or some other implement of dark death?"

DAVE. Excuse me?

HENRY. A line from *Medea*.

DAVE. It's just her term paper.

HENRY. She should be in class. She should hand it in herself.

DAVE. I think she's — a little mad at you, sir.

HENRY. Mad? At me? Because I want her to learn? Oh dear. Would you tell her, please, that the quest for truth and beauty is a slow and painful climb, and she shouldn't bite the hand that leads her. *(His little pun.)*

DAVE. I'll — tell her something.

HENRY. Good. Meanwhile, I'll take that paper, in hopes she soon will return to the fold.

DAVE. Thank you, sir.

HENRY. *(Opening the envelope, sliding the paper out far enough to read the title.)* "Tragic Irony in Sophocles' *Antigone*." A good, no-nonsense title.

DAVE. I'll tell her, sir. *(He starts off.)*

HENRY. *(Pulling the paper out of the envelope.)* Lovely looking paper ... Well typed.

DAVE. Mmm.

HENRY. Is this an electric typewriter?

DAVE. No actually, it's a word processor.

HENRY. She can't come to class, but she seems to have found time to form a relationship with a computer.

DAVE. Actually, I did the typing, sir.

HENRY. Well let's hope the contents are as attractive as the form. *(He starts to thumb through the papers.)*

DAVE. I'll be going, then. *(He starts off.)*

HENRY. *(As he reads; calling out.)* Oh, ah, Mr. —

DAVE. *(Stopping; turning.)* Dave.

HENRY. Do you have a moment?

DAVE. Well I—

HENRY. Would you be so kind as to accompany me to my office?

DAVE. Me?

HENRY. If you would.

DAVE. Now?

HENRY. If you'd be so kind. *(He turns and crosses slowly toward his office, still reading the paper. Dave hesitates a moment, and then follows. Henry enters his office, and sits at his desk, still reading. Dave stands in the doorway. As he reads, gesturing vaguely.)* Please sit down, Mr. ... ah ...

DAVE. Dave.

HENRY. Sit down, please.

DAVE. Thank you. *(He sits on the edge of the chair. Henry continues to read. Dave watches him.)*

HENRY. *(As he reads.)* This ... appears to be ... an excellent paper.

DAVE. Is it?

HENRY. *(Thumbing through to the end.)* Even a cursory glance tells me it's first-rate.

DAVE. I'll tell her, sir.

HENRY. I've been around a long time. I've taught this course a good many years. I know a good paper when I see one, and I see one here.

DAVE. *(Almost at the door.)* That's great, sir.

HENRY. *(Quietly.)* Who wrote it?

DAVE. Huh?

HENRY. Who wrote this paper?

DAVE. Judy wrote it.

HENRY. No she didn't. I've also been around long enough to know that. She wrote a promising little essay for me at the start of the semester. She wrote a rather breathless hour exam. But she did not write this. She is not yet capable of the care and commitment I see emerging here.

DAVE. Maybe she's changed, sir.

HENRY. Ah. Then I would like to discuss this paper with her. Would you get her, please?

DAVE. I think she's rehearsing, sir.

HENRY. Then I must ask you to seek her out. Tell her I am passionate to engage in an intensive discussion with a kindred classicist.

DAVE. Sir ...

HENRY. You might also tell her, *en passant,* that I think this is plagiarism, pure and simple. She has tried to pass off as her own the work of somebody else. This is an offense punishable, according to the rules, by ... *(He has found the college rule book and is already thumbing through it. He finds his place.)* "Automatic failure of the course involved."

DAVE. Sir ...

HENRY. *(Reading.)* "*And,* after due deliberation by the Discipline Committee, possible expulsion from the University." *(Pause. He looks at Dave.)*

DAVE. *(Quietly.)* Oh boy.

HENRY. You might also be interested in the fact that ... *(He reads again from the book.)* "persons aiding or contributing to a plagiaristic act will similarly be charged and punished." *(Looks up.)* You personally might be interested in that, Mr. — ?

DAVE. Appleton.

HENRY. Well I'm not going to press charges against you, Mr. Appleton.

DAVE. Sir —

HENRY. Nor am I going to press charges against Miss Miller. Believe it or not, I would hate to prevent her from graduating. I would simply ask you to tell her to make an appointment at her earliest convenience, so that I may explain to her why, in the world of scholarship and learning, plagiarism is a dark and bloody crime. *(Dave stands at the door.)* That's all I have to say. You may go.

DAVE. She didn't write it.

HENRY. *(Infinitely patient.)* Yes I know. That's what I've been saying.

DAVE. No, I mean she doesn't even know about it.

HENRY. Doesn't know?

DAVE. She still wants her play to be her paper. *(Pause.)*

HENRY. Then who wrote this?

DAVE. I did.

HENRY. Unbeknownst to her?

DAVE. Yes, sir.

HENRY. Hoping I'd give it a good grade, and she'd go along with it, and the problem would be solved?

DAVE. I don't know what I hoped. *(Pause.)*

HENRY. *(Looking at paper again.)* And where did you get this paper? From some other student at some other college? From one of those companies who accept money and do your research?

DAVE. No! I wrote it myself.

HENRY. I don't believe that.

DAVE. Well I did.

HENRY. How could you? You're not in my course.

DAVE. I still wrote it. *(Pause. Henry looks at the paper, looks at Dave.)*

HENRY. Sit down, please. *(Dave does. Henry is now all business.)* Name three plays by Sophocles beside the *Antigone.*

DAVE. *Oedipus Rex, Oedipus at Colonnus ... Ajax.*

HENRY. Describe Antigone's geneology.

DAVE. Her father was Oedipus. Her mother, Jocasta. Her sister was Ismene. She had two brothers, Eteocles and Polynices. *(Pause.)* Who killed each other. *(Pause.)* Fighting. *(Pause.)* For the throne. *(Pause.)* Of Thebes. *(Pause.)*

HENRY. And what, briefly, do you think *is* the "Tragic Irony in Sophocles' *Antigone*"?

DAVE. I don't think it's Antigone's tragedy at all. I think it's Creon's.

HENRY. And why do you think that?

DAVE. Because she at least wins her point in the end.

HENRY. She dies.

DAVE. But she wins. He loses. Everything. The Gods are much more unfair to him. *(Pause.)*

HENRY. You're very good.

DAVE. Thank you.

HENRY. Where did you learn all this?

DAVE. I read the play.

HENRY. *(Indicating paper.)* No. There's more here than just that.

DAVE. My grandfather liked the Greeks.

HENRY. Was he an academic?

DAVE. No. He just liked the classics. He spent most of his spare time in the library, reading the Greeks.

HENRY. And he taught you?

DAVE. Right. And I kept it up when I had time.

HENRY. I could never get my own son to read anything but science fiction.

DAVE. That's what my dad reads. *(They laugh together.)*

HENRY. Why have you never taken a course from me?

DAVE. I couldn't fit it into my schedule.

HENRY. What's your major?

DAVE. Chemistry.

HENRY. Better worlds through chemistry, eh.

DAVE. Actually, my grades aren't too good.

HENRY. They'd be good in the classics.

DAVE. Not many jobs out there in that.

HENRY. Still, you should take my course.

DAVE. I wish I could.

HENRY. We could do a special seminar together. Study one play in depth. I'm fascinated with the *Antigone*. We could really dig in, you and I, next fall.

DAVE. I'm supposed to graduate this spring, sir.

HENRY. Oh dear ... Then perhaps we might meet in the afternoon, from here on in. A small tutorial.

DAVE. I can't, sir. I'm on the track team.

HENRY. The track team? Splendid! The Greeks invented competitive sport!

DAVE. I know.

HENRY. *Hygies psyche meta somatos hygious.*

DAVE. Excuse me?

HENRY. We'll shift to Latin: *Mens sana in corpore sano.*

DAVE. *(Trying to translate.)* Sane mind ...

HENRY. Sound mind in a sound body. The Tenth Satire by Juvenal.

DAVE. Juvenal ... Tenth ...

HENRY. You don't by any chance throw the discus, do you? No, that would be too much.

DAVE. I just run the Four Hundred.

HENRY. Ah. Fleet of foot. A true Greek. "Skilled in all ways of contending."

DAVE. Thank you, sir.

HENRY. Well, then, I wonder if I might keep this fine paper long enough for Mrs. Murphy to make a Xerox copy.

DAVE. Sure. *(He gets up to leave.)*

HENRY. Just to remind me occasionally of what a good student can do.

DAVE. Sure. *(He starts for the door. At this point, Judy enters at another part of the stage. She sits on a bench, and waits impatiently, as if in a waiting room.)*

HENRY. You must be very fond of Miss Miller.

DAVE. I am.

HENRY. To have written this for her.

DAVE. I liked writing it.

HENRY. Will you be seeing her soon?

DAVE. I think so.

HENRY. Would you remind her that she and I have yet to resolve

34

our difficulties?

DAVE. She's stubborn, sir.

HENRY. I give you permission to help her. Be her tutor. See that she gets some small awareness of Greek tragedy.

DAVE. She thinks she already has, sir.

HENRY. But she *hasn't!* She sees answers, solutions, revisions. Tell her there are things beyond the world of management which are profoundly unmanageable!

DAVE. She wouldn't listen, sir.

HENRY. Then she and I are on a collision course.

DAVE. I'm afraid so, sir. *(Dave starts for the door again.)*

HENRY. One more minute, please. *(Dave stops.)* Appleton, you said your name was?

DAVE. That's right.

HENRY. English, I suppose.

DAVE. Originally.

HENRY. The English love the classics.

DAVE. Yes.

HENRY. And Miss Miller's Jewish.

DAVE. That's right.

HENRY. May I speak classicist to classicist?

DAVE. Yeah. Sure.

HENRY. What you are witnessing here, Mr. Appleton, is once again the age-old clash between Athens and Jerusalem.

DAVE. I don't get you, sir.

HENRY. Read Tertullian. Third century, A.D. "What is Athens to Jerusalem, or Jerusalem to Athens?" There it all is. The private conscience versus the communal obligation. Jew versus Greek. Miss Miller versus me.

DAVE. You think so?

HENRY. I do, but they tell me I shouldn't.

DAVE. It seems a little ... exaggerated, sir.

HENRY. You're probably right. *(Henry gets up; takes his arm.)* Come, I'll walk with you down the hall. Plato and Aristotle, strolling through the colonnades of academe. We'll discuss simply Sophocles.

DAVE. O.K.

HENRY. *(As they go.)* And I hope Miss Miller appreciates this grand gesture you made on her behalf.

DAVE. God, I hope she never finds out about it. *(They go out as Diana comes on, carrying a folder. Judy gets up expectantly.)*

JUDY. Well?

DIANA. The meeting's over.

JUDY. And?

DIANA. *(Deep breath.)* The Grievance Committee voted against you, Judy.

JUDY. *Against?*

DIANA. I'm sorry. *(They move into her office.)*

JUDY. Did the students on the committee vote against me?

DIANA. I can't reveal the specific vote.

JUDY. How about you? How did you vote?

DIANA. I abstained, of course. Since I was presenting your case.

JUDY. How would you have voted? If you could have? *(Pause.)*

DIANA. Against.

JUDY. What?!

DIANA. I put your case as fairly as I could, Judy. Really. But your argument simply didn't hold. The committee felt you were asking them to violate the integrity of the classroom. You want them to intrude on a principle that goes back to the Middle Ages.

JUDY. But other people do it all the time! There's a guy in Geology who got partial credit for skiing down Mount Washington!

DIANA. I know ...

JUDY. And there's a girl who passed her Chemistry lab by cooking a crabmeat casserole.

DIANA. I know that, and I think it's disgraceful. But those are other instructors. We cannot dictate standards to *any* professor. You signed up for Greek tragedy. You bought the books. You read the syllabus. You agreed in effect to submit to the rules. There it is.

JUDY. There it is. Everyone seems to be backing off these days.

You, my family, now the committee.

DIANA. Oh, Judy ...

JUDY. *(Almost in tears.)* I guess I'm doomed to be alone.

DIANA. What about all those people working on your play?

JUDY. It's just extra curricular to them. I'm the one who's really on the line.

DIANA. Well what about that boy you go with?

JUDY. Oh, he just loves me, that's all.

DIANA. *(Lighting a cigarette.)* Well I'm sorry, Judy. I did what I could.

JUDY. Please don't smoke!

DIANA. I'm sorry.

JUDY. I think I'm allergic to it.

DIANA. All right, Judy.

JUDY. And it violates my air space.

DIANA. *(Putting cigarettes away.)* All right, all right. *(Pause.)*

JUDY. So what do I do?

DIANA. I told you: he's offered a C.

JUDY. I'm beyond a C.

DIANA. Beyond?

JUDY. I can't settle for a C.

DIANA. Then you won't graduate.

JUDY. Not in June. No.

DIANA. That's ridiculous!

JUDY. I'll make it up in summer school with that course on comedy where all they do is study *Annie Hall.* You can mail me my degree in September.

DIANA. That makes me a little angry, Judy. You told me you wanted to stand up with your class.

JUDY. I'm standing up, all right.

DIANA. But you'll lose your job! It depends on your graduating.

JUDY. I'll find another.

DIANA. That's not so easy these days.

JUDY. What's a job anyway? Is it the most important thing in the world? I suppose this is a hopelessly middle-class thing to say, but am I supposed to live and die over a job? Do you? You've been here a long time, worked your way up, now you're Dean of the whole department. Is that *it?* Are you in heaven now? Aren't there other things in your life beside your job?

DIANA. *(Taken aback.)* Of course there are, Judy ...

JUDY. I mean, that's all I cared about, once upon a time. A *job.* I couldn't wait until I was scampering up and down Wall Street in my gray and white Adidas and a new suit from Saks, with my little leather briefcase swinging by my side. Meeting men for lunch and women for dinner, and both in the Health Club afterwards. A co-op on the East Side with a VCR and an answering machine with a funny message. Weekends at Sugarbush and Vineyard. Vacations in the Bahamas and France. Nailing down forty or fifty thou per annum within three years. Moving onward and upward through the corridors of power until I get an office with a corner view where I can look down on millions of women scampering up and down Wall Street in their gray and white Adidas.

DIANA. That's not the worst thing in the world!

JUDY. Isn't it? I'm not so sure. I'm beginning to think it's a con deal. All us women now killing ourselves to do those things that a lot of men decided not to do twenty years ago. I mean, here we are, the organization women, punching the clock, flashing the credit card, smoking our lungs out, while the really smart men are off making furniture or playing the clarinet or something. Look at you. Do you really want to be Dean, or are you just making some sort of feminist statement?

DIANA. Let's leave me out of this, please.

JUDY. Well all I know is I'm not so hung up on "The Job" any-more. It just seems like more of the same. More of what I did at Andover and at Westport Junior High before that. More of what I've done every summer, with my creative camps and Internships and my Special Summer Projects. Touching all the bases, following all the rules, ever since I can remember. And now here I am, about to graduate, or rather *not* graduate, because I've come up with the first vaguely unselfish idea I've ever had in my life, and this place, this institution — in which my family has invested at least seventy thousand dollars — won't give me credit for it.

DIANA. A C is a decent grade, Judy. We used to call it a gentleman's C.

JUDY. Well I'm no gentleman. *(She starts out.)*

DIANA. Judy ... One more thing. *(Judy stops, turns.)*

JUDY. What?

DIANA. The Provost sat in on the Grievance Committee meeting.

JUDY. And?

DIANA. After it was over, he took me aside. He asked me to ask you a question.

JUDY. Go ahead.

DIANA. ... The Provost wondered if your difficulty with Professor Harper has anything to do with ... ethnic issues.

JUDY. Say again?

DIANA. A student has recently complained that Professor Harper is anti-Semitic?

JUDY. Anti-Se*mit*ic?

DIANA. That's the complaint.

JUDY. Anti-Semitic? It's probably that Talmudic type who sits in the front row and argues about everything. I bet he wears his yarmulke even in the shower.

DIANA. Ah, but you don't feel that way?

JUDY. No way.

DIANA. Oh, Judy, I'm so glad to hear it.

JUDY. I never even thought of it.

DIANA. Good. Then I'll tell the Provost.

JUDY. I mean should I worry about that? My grandmother says you have to watch out for that sort of thing at all times.

DIANA. Yes well, times change.

JUDY. Unless it's there, and I didn't see it.

DIANA. No, no ...

JUDY. I mean, maybe I'm so assimilated into white-bread middle-class America that it passed me right by. Maybe I should reexamine this whole issue with that in mind. Thanks a lot, Dean! *(She goes out.)*

DIANA. *(Calling after her.)* Judy! Judy! ... Oh God! *(She makes up her mind, opens a desk drawer, takes out a small tape recorder which she slams onto the desk. She pushes the buttons determinedly and then begins to dictate, pacing around her office as she smokes. Dictating.)* Monica, please type a letter to the Provost ... Dear Walter ... I herewith submit my resignation as Dean, to be effective at the end of this school year. I find I long to return to the clear lines and concrete issues of the classroom. I especially yearn to resume my studies of Jane Austen, and the subordinate role of women in the 18th century. I will miss, of course, the sense of bustle and activity I've found here in Administration. There's something to be said, after all, for the friendships which come from working closely with other people during regular hours — among which I count my friendship with the other Deans, and you, Walter, and Monica, my fine assistant ... Indeed, in someways, I dread retreating to the hermetic world of bickering colleagues, sullen students, hopeless meetings, long hours of preparation ... *(She slows down.)* ... the loneliness of the library ... the meals alone ... the sense that something more important is going on everywhere else in the world ... *(Long pause.)* Just type a rough draft of this, Monica. I'll look at it tomorrow. *(She clicks off the tape recorder, puts it back in her desk. Dave enters in a track suit, starts doing stretch exercises. Diana crosses to doorway, calls off.)* Monica, see if you can locate Professor Harper ... *(Then she takes some computer printout sheets out of her briefcase and begins to go over them at her desk as the lights dim on her. The lights come up more fully on Dave, doing stretch exercises. We hear the distant sounds of students cheering. Judy comes on. It is by now late enough in the spring so she doesn't wear a jacket.)*

JUDY. Dave ... *(She hugs him from behind.)*

DAVE. *(Through his stretches; pantingly.)* Hi ...

JUDY. Am I bothering you?

DAVE. *(Grunting; stretching.)* Yes ... But that's O.K.

JUDY. I just want to tell you something, David.

DAVE. *(Still exercising.)* Uh oh. When it's David, it's serious.

JUDY. I just want to tell you not to memorize any more of those speeches.

DAVE. Thank God.

JUDY. I'm changing everything.

DAVE. Again?

JUDY. I'm starting all over. From scratch.

DAVE. Why?

JUDY. I didn't like what we had. I can do better.

DAVE. Yeah?

JUDY. Now I'm on a totally different track. I mean, it's still *Antigone.* But I'm adding a whole new dimension.

DAVE. Are you throwing in acid rain?

JUDY. *(Laughing.)* No. I'm onto something much deeper. *(A whistle is heard offstage. Dave starts off.)*

DAVE. There's the Four Hundred. I've got to go.

JUDY. So throw away the old stuff.

DAVE. Is there a lot new to learn?

JUDY. Mostly for me.

DAVE. Can you tell me where you're taking it?

JUDY. Well I'm striving for a more natural style.

DAVE. Way to go.

JUDY. And I'm connecting my attack on nuclear armaments with the issue of meaningful work.

DAVE. Excellent.

JUDY. And I'm making Antigone Jewish. *(She goes off. Another whistle from offstage. He looks after her, then runs off the opposite way as ... the lights come up on Diana, who is still at her desk, working on print-out sheets. After a moment, Henry appears in the doorway. He watches her affectionately for a moment.)*

HENRY. *(Finally.)* Woman at her work. I am reminded of Penelope at her loom.

DIANA. *(Looking up; quickly putting away the sheets.)* Come in, Henry.

HENRY. *(Coming in.)* What a magnificent office, Diana! What corporate dimensions! *(As Diana puts her cigarette out.)* Thank you ... A view of the Charles! The spires of Harvard dimly seen up the river! How different it is from the monkish cells assigned to those of us who teach.

DIANA. You've been here before, Henry.

HENRY. Never. I've scrupulously avoided all official contact with the bureaucracy, except on my own turf. I wouldn't be here now, dear Diana, but for a series of rather frantic telephone messages left under my door. *(He takes a stack of pink slips out of his pocket, reads.)* Call the Dean ... See the Dean ... Please call or see the Dean.

DIANA. Sit down, Henry.

HENRY. *(Sitting.)* I will, but I must warn you I have very little time. We are now deep in the last plays of Euripides, particularly the *Bacchae*, which I continually find to be one of the more profoundly disturbing works of man. He has an even darker vision than Sophocles.

DIANA. Well maybe I've got some news that will cheer you up, Henry.

HENRY. Beware of Deans bearing gifts.

DIANA. Remember that grant you applied for two years ago?

HENRY. Ah yes. To go to Greece. To see the restorations at Epidaurus. *(Pause.)* And to restore a ruin or two in my own life.

DIANA. Well you've got that grant now, Henry.

HENRY. Now?

DIANA. I've been talking to the Provost. He's giving you next year off. All year. At full pay.

HENRY. Are you serious?

DIANA. I'm always serious, Henry. That's my problem, in case you ever notice. *(Pause.)*

HENRY. Why suddenly now?

DIANA. Ours not to reason why, Henry.

HENRY. I begged for that leave two years ago. I practically fell to my knees and supplicated the Provost like old Priam before Achilles. I thought if Elsa and I could just get away ...

DIANA. Call her. Tell her you've lucked out, at long last.

HENRY. It's too late. She's ... found someone. Apparently they sit and hold hands and watch television. Anyway, she wants a divorce.

DIANA. I am sorry.

HENRY. No, no, it's good. It's very good. The other shoe has dropped. Finally.

DIANA. Take one of your children then. Give them a trip.

HENRY. They wouldn't come. *(Pause.)* They have their own lives. *(Pause.)* Such as they are. *(Quietly.)* I'll go alone. *(Pause; he looks at her.)* Unless you'd come with me.

DIANA. Henry!

HENRY. Why not? Take a sabbatical. You're overdue.

DIANA. You mean, just — blip out into the blue Aegean?

HENRY. Exactly! Spend a naughty year abroad with an old satyr. Tell you what, I'd even let you smoke.

DIANA. I think I'd give it up if I went abroad.

HENRY. Then there we are!

DIANA. Oh gosh! To get away! To see something else besides these — walls! Just think, Henry ... *(She stops.)* Just think. *(Pause. Sadly.)* It wouldn't work, Henry.

HENRY. It might.

DIANA. It already didn't, Henry. On that strange weekend in that gloomy hotel during the M.L.A. conference.

HENRY. That was a lovely weekend.

DIANA. It was not.

HENRY. Dido and Aeneas in their enchanted cave ...

DIANA. Oh Henry, *please!*

HENRY. What's the matter?

DIANA. Dido, Penelope, Clytemnestra! I am not a *myth*, Henry! I am not a *met*aphor!

HENRY. My dear lady ...

DIANA. No, no, I'm *me*, Henry! I live and breathe in my own right! Do you know anything about my *life?* Do you know where I live? Do you know I have a daughter in Junior High?

HENRY. Of course I know you have ...

DIANA. What's her name, Henry? What's my daughter's *name?* It's not Electra and it's not Athena and it's not ...

HENRY. Let me think ...

DIANA. You don't *know*, Henry. And you don't know that my mother died last semester, and you don't know that I used to play the French horn. You don't *see* me, Henry. You don't see anyone.

43

In your mind, everything is an example of something else! I suppose it's called stereotyping, but whatever it is, I don't like it, Henry! It makes me feel insignificant and unreal.

HENRY. Diana, dear friend ... *(He moves toward her.)*

DIANA. No, now stay away from me, Henry. Don't touch me. Go to *Greece*, for God's sake! Find some young woman — excuse me, some sea nymph — who will throw herself into your arms on the topless shores of Mykenos. Really. Just go. *(Pause.)*

HENRY. Tell the Provost I'll take a raincheck.

DIANA. A raincheck?

HENRY. Maybe in a year or two. When my life is more in order.

DIANA. It doesn't work that way, Henry. It's now or not at all.

HENRY. Then I'll have to forego it.

DIANA. Oh Henry ...

HENRY. At this point in my life, I need my classes. Strange as that may seem. *(He starts out.)* And now, if you'll excuse me, the *Bacchae* call me to the dance.

DIANA. Henry! *(He stops.)* Other things go on in this university at the end of the school year besides discussions of the *Bacchae.*

HENRY. *(Stopping, turning.)* Such as?

DIANA. *(Taking the computer printouts from her desk.)* Well, for example, Henry, there's something called preregistration, when students give an indication of what courses they'd like to take next fall.

HENRY. The annual body count.

DIANA. *(Indicating sheets.)* Exactly, Henry. And we in the Humanities are down.

HENRY. We are always down. We are doomed to be down. We live in an age where a book — a good book — is as obsolete as an Aeolian harp. All the more reason to keep standards *up.*

DIANA. You, particularly, are down, Henry. *(Pause.)*

HENRY. How many did I get?

DIANA. Two.

HENRY. Two? Two next fall? Two students to take through the

entire rise and fall of the Roman Empire.

DIANA. Two, Henry.

HENRY. How many for my elective on Plato?

DIANA. Four.

HENRY. Four. Two for Rome, four for Plato. Six students, next fall, out of over four thousand, have shown some interest in the classical tradition. This, in a country founded by Washington and Jefferson and Madison precisely to reestablish that tradition.

DIANA. Shakespeare, on the other hand, is up.

HENRY. I must say, Diana, I fail to understand why students choose what they do. They land on courses like starlings on a telephone wire. It seems totally random.

DIANA. The Provost is cancelling all undergraduate courses with an enrollment of less than five, Henry.

HENRY. What?

DIANA. The Provost is cancelling your courses.

HENRY. He has no right!

DIANA. He has every right. It's a budgetary thing. There are clear rules about it. Jack Edward's seminar on Racine goes. Sally Weiskopf's section on Keats. The history department lost the entire seventeenth century.

HENRY. I'll talk to him. These things can change. Students can sign up in the fall.

DIANA. He's laid down the law, Henry. Jack Edwards has already gone up and been refused. *(Pause.)*

HENRY. Then I'll teach something else.

DIANA. Such as what, Henry?

HENRY. Dante. I'll teach Dante. I'm beginning to get a new understanding of Hell.

DIANA. Bill Brindisi's got Dante.

HENRY. Shakespeare, then. I'll do a section of Shakespeare.

DIANA. You don't like Shakespeare.

HENRY. Of course I like Shakephere. He's just a bit ... messy, that's all. And a bit over-picked. I refuse to spend an entire class focussing on the button image in *King Lear*. I'll do the Roman plays: *Julius Caesar, Coriolanus ...*

DIANA. Jane Tillotson's got Shakespeare, Henry. All of him.

HENRY. All right then, what? Tolstoy? Joyce? I'm an educated man. I can do anything. Give me the freshman course — Introduction to Literature. I'll take it over. I'll muster that motley crew of junior instructors who teach it. We'll begin with the *Iliad*, and stride down the centuries, concluding with Conrad.

DIANA. I think they *start* with Conrad in that course, Henry.

HENRY. Oh really? Well, we'll change that. We'll —

DIANA. Henry. *(Pause.)* The Provost doesn't want you to teach. At all.

HENRY. Why not?

DIANA. He thinks your courses are becoming ... problematic, Henry.

HENRY. The *Antigone* thing?

DIANA. And the anti-Semitic thing.

HENRY. I have scrupulously avoided anything controversial in my class.

DIANA. Apparently she hasn't, in her play. I hear it's more and more about being Jewish, and more and more about you.

HENRY. *(Quietly, with increasing anger.)* There is a law as old as Solon which allows a man to confront his accusers. I want to meet her, right now, in front of the Provost, and you, and Ariel Sharon, if he wants to be there!

DIANA. The Provost already met with her, Henry.

HENRY. And what did she say?

DIANA. Nothing! Everything! I don't know! He said it was all very general ... He said you both deserve each other. He said if he didn't have the alumni breathing down his neck, he'd turn you both loose in the ring, and the hell with it. But right now, all he wants to do is get her graduated and you out of the country, so that things can simmer *down*. Now go to *Greece*, Henry, and enjoy it!

HENRY. And when I come back, he'll suggest early retirement.

DIANA. He might.

HENRY. He'll sweeten the pie. Buy me off with a few impressive benefits.

46

DIANA. You've been here a long time, Henry. I think they'd be very generous.

HENRY. I want to teach, Diana.

DIANA. I know.

HENRY. I need to teach.

DIANA. I know, I know ...

HENRY. It's what I do.

DIANA. Henry, my old colleague ...

HENRY. I am a classical scholar. I trained at Harvard. I have written three good books. I know a great deal, and I have to teach what I know, and I'm only good when I'm teaching it! My wife has left me, my children have scattered, I have nothing else but this! I have to teach, Diana. Have to. Or I'm dead.

DIANA. You need students, Henry.

HENRY. Then I'll have to get them, won't I? *(He goes off. Diana sits there for a moment, then opens her purse, takes out a pack of cigarettes. She shakes it, but it's empty. She gets up, and begins to walk toward the wings, calling out sweetly as she goes.)*

DIANA. Monica? ... Did you bring any cigarettes in today? ... Because if you did, even though you're down to your last one, I intend to get it, Monica. I intend to wrestle you to the ground! *(She goes off, as Judy comes on. She leans against a pillar in a rather theatrical pose and recites her lines, referring only occasionally to a script she carries, in her hand.)*

JUDY. "So Creon has determined I go to jail. I wonder if this is happening because I'm Jewish. I don't mean simply that Creon's prejudiced — though he probably is. I mean more because of me. Maybe it's built into my Jewish blood to rise up against the Creons of this world. All I know is for the first time in my life I've felt in tune with something larger than myself. I've been to the library lately. I've studied my roots. And I've learned how often we Jews have stood our ground against injustice. Pharaoh and Philistine, Hittite and Herod have fallen before us. Roman generals and Spanish Inquisitors, Venetian businessmen and Russian Cossacks, Nazis, Arabs, McCarthyites — all the arrogant authorities of this world have tried to subdue us. And when we protest, they throw us into jail. Well, what's jail these days? Maybe this is a jail right here. This so-called ivory tower. This labyrinth of curricular obligations. This festering nest of overpaid administrators. This rotten pit of dry and exhausted pedants. This winter camp which capitalism creates to keep its children off the job market. What job market? Where are the jobs? Where is there decent work in an economy so devoted to nonessential goods and destructive weapons?" *(Dave comes on.)*

DAVE. Judy —

JUDY. Wait. I'm almost done. *(She continues to recite.)* "Or maybe this whole damn country is a jail. Maybe we're all prisoners. Prisoners of these oppressive corporations, who capture us with their advertising, chain us to their products, and work us forever in meaningless jobs to pay for things we shouldn't even want."

DAVE. Judy. It's important.

JUDY. Hold it. *(She takes a deep breath.)* "And to protect this prison, this fortress America, this so-called way of life, we arm ourselves with weapons which, if they're used, could ten times over destroy the world, blot out the past, and turn the future into a desolate blank. Are we so sure we're right? Is life in these United States so great? Would the homeless hordes on the streets of New York agree? Would the hungry blacks in the South? Would the migrant workers breaking their backs to feed us go along with it? Oh God, Lysander, this might be a terrible thing to say, but I don't think our country is worth dying for any more. The world at large is worth dying for, not just us."

DAVE. Wow! That's tremendous.

JUDY. Thank you. *) Pause.)*

DAVE. *(Quietly.)* He wants to see you.

JUDY. The Provost? I know. I have a meeting with him in half an hour.

DAVE. No, *Harper! Harper* wants to see you.

JUDY. Harper?

DAVE. He called me at the lab.

JUDY. How come he called *you?*

DAVE. I don't know ... I guess he knew I knew you. Anyway, he said he watched the rehearsal last night.

JUDY. *What?*

DAVE. He was there. And he wants to talk to you about it.

JUDY. Oh God. What did he think?

DAVE. Didn't say. *(The lights begin to come up on Henry's office, as Henry comes in, settles at his desk.)*

JUDY. Oh Lord, he must have hated it. All that Creon stuff I put in. Well, maybe it'll do him good.

DAVE. He said he'd be in his office all afternoon. You better see him.

JUDY. *(Putting on lip gloss.)* I might. Then again I might not. First, of course, I have a major meeting with the Provost. *(She starts out.)*

DAVE. *(Calling after Judy.)* Hey, you're quite the Queen Bee around here these days.

JUDY. I'm another Antigone.

DAVE. Antigone dies in the end, remember.

JUDY. That's the old version. Mine ends happily ever after. *(She goes off.)*

DAVE. *(Calling after her.)* Ever hear of *hubris*, Judy? Know what that word means ... *(He sees she's gone; speaks to himself.)* Pride. Overweening pride. For example, take a man whose father gives him a chemistry set when he's eight years old. This man takes Chemistry in high school, and majors in it in college. What makes this man think he can graduate if he doesn't study? What makes this man think he can find a job if he doesn't graduate? What makes this man stand around, talking to himself, when his final exam in Chemistry starts in five minutes, and he doesn't know the stuff at *all?* Pride, that's what. *Hubris.* Which leads to tragedy every time. *(He goes off grimly as the lights come up on Henry in his office. After a moment, Judy comes in.)*

JUDY. You wanted to see me, Professor Harper?

HENRY. *(Jumping up.)* Ah. Miss Miller. Yes. *(Indicates a chair.)* Please. *(Judy comes in.)* How well you look.

JUDY. Thank you.

HENRY. I am reminded of a line from the *Andromache:* "I now wear different robes."

JUDY. I don't know that one.

HENRY. No matter. You look lovely. Life on the wicked stage becomes you.

JUDY. Thanks. *(She sits.)*

HENRY. Yes, well, now I have recently had the opportunity to watch you practice your play.

JUDY. You mean, re*hearse.*

HENRY. Yes. Rehearse. Last night, in fact. I happen to know old Bill, who's the custodian of the Spingler Auditorium, and he took me up to the back of the balcony and let me sit there unobtrusively and watch you rehearse your play.

JUDY. I heard.

HENRY. Oh yes? Well that's where I was. All evening. *(Pause.)* I found it ... *(This is tough for him.)* Interesting. *(Pause.)* Quite interesting. *(Pause.)* The crude poetry, the naive theatricality ...

JUDY. Thank you.

HENRY. Your work also demonstrated an earnestness and commitment which I found ... refreshing, in a world which seems too often concerned only with the meaning of meaning.

JUDY. You mean, you *liked* it? *(Pause.)*

HENRY. I ... admired it.

JUDY. Well thank you very much! I appreciate that.

HENRY. I have decided it may substitute after all for your term paper.

JUDY. That's great!

HENRY. Miss Miller, you might be interested to know that Sophocles himself was a practical man of the theatre. Not only did he write his plays, but he directed most of them, and sometimes acted in them as well, just as you are doing.

JUDY. Really?

HENRY. Absolutely. And according to Aristotle — this might amuse you — he actually danced in a lost play of his called *Nausicaa.* He danced. He danced the part of a young woman playing ball.

JUDY. No kidding! That makes me feel very proud!

HENRY. Then I wonder if you would play ball with *me*, Miss Miller.

50

JUDY. What do you mean?

HENRY. Well now, last night, I noticed a number of people scurrying about, assisting with your production.

JUDY. Yes ...

HENRY. Good, practical souls, hard at work. I mean, not only did I notice your personal and particular friend ...

JUDY. Dave ...

HENRY. Yes, Dave. A fine, stalwart young man. I noticed him. But I also noticed other actors, and that odd cluster of people pretending to be the chorus.

JUDY. Right ...

HENRY. And then I hear there's to be an orchestra ...

JUDY. A group. A combo, really ...

HENRY. Well how many do you think are involved, in toto?

JUDY. In toto?

HENRY. Altogether.

JUDY. Oh ... maybe ... thirty-five.

HENRY. And of course not all of them will graduate this year, will they?

JUDY. No. Some. Not all.

HENRY. Miss Miller, I wonder if you would announce to everyone in your production that I'm planning to give a special seminar next fall.

JUDY. Special seminar?

HENRY. On the Greeks. And since these students have all been working on your *Antigone*, I'll give them the inside track. They *must*, however — you must tell them this — they *must* let the Dean's office know they're interested, so we'll have some indication of preenrollment.

JUDY. Professor Harper, I'm not sure they'd want to —

HENRY. Oh yes they would. Tell them this course will be — how shall I put it? — "project-oriented." They can put on plays. They can make models of the Parthenon. They can draw maps of the Peloponnesian Peninsula, I don't care!

JUDY. That doesn't sound like you, Professor Harper.

HENRY. Oh yes, yes. And tell them I'll grade it Pass/Fail, if they want. And I'll have very few papers. No papers at all, really, if that's what they want. Because the important thing is not papers, is it, it's the Greeks! We'll be studying the Greeks next year, that's the thing! We'll still be reading and discussing those fine old plays. We'll still be holding onto the heart of Western Civilization. That's what we'll be doing, Miss Miller, and you will have helped us do it! *(Pause.)*

JUDY. You mean you want students next year.

HENRY. Yes, frankly, I do. *(Pause.)*

JUDY. Wow!

HENRY. There it is.

JUDY. I always thought we had to go through you. I never thought you had to go through *us*.

HENRY. Well we do.

JUDY. You really *need* us, don't you? You have to have us.

HENRY. Without you, we'd die.

JUDY. I never knew that before.

HENRY. Now you do. *(Pause.)* So will you tell them about the course?

JUDY. Yes I will.

HENRY. And you'll encourage them to come?

JUDY. I'll tell them, Professor Harper. I'll let them choose.

HENRY. But you won't ... undercut me?

JUDY. No, I won't do that.

HENRY. And you'll remind them to sign up immediately. So the administration will know.

JUDY. I'll do all that, sir. I mean, you have a right to live, too, after all.

HENRY. You're magnanimous in victory, Miss Miller.

JUDY. Thank you, sir.

HENRY. Now, before we turn to the crass topic or grades, suppose we celebrate the conclusion of these negotiations. *(Opens his drawer again, takes out a sherry bottle and two murky glasses.)* I keep this sherry around for those rare occasions when a fellow scholar stops by.

JUDY. Oh I don't —

HENRY. *(Pouring.)* Please. It's important. Old Odysseus and the nymph Calypso, in Book Five of the *Odyssey,* sharing a glass before they say goodbye. *(He hands her her glass, raises his in a toast.)* To peace and reconciliation. *(They click glasses and drink.)* Doesn't that hit the spot?

JUDY. Actually, it does.

HENRY. Have some more.

JUDY. Oh, well. No. I mean, all right. *(He pours her more, and a touch more for himself. Judy gets up.)* You know, I was just thinking, Professor Harper ...

HENRY. *(His little joke.)* That's always a good sign.

JUDY. No, seriously, I was thinking that you and I are basically very much alike.

HENRY. Ah? And how so?

JUDY. I mean we both see too big a picture.

HENRY. Elucidate, please.

JUDY. Sure. I mean, there you are, always talking about the Greeks versus the Jews, and here I am, talking about the Jews versus all authority.

HENRY. I see.

JUDY. Maybe we should both scale things down.

HENRY. Maybe we should. *(Settling back in his chair.)* In any case, I think you can count on receiving a B in my course, Miss Miller.

JUDY. A B.

HENRY. A strong B. A solid B. A B which leans longingly toward a B plus.

JUDY. I was kind of hoping I'd get an A.

HENRY. I don't think your work quite warrants an A, Miss Miller.

JUDY. You don't think so?

HENRY. Let's reserve the A's for Sophocles, shall we? It gives us something to go for. *(Pause.)*

JUDY. That's cool.

HENRY. I take it you agree.

JUDY. I guess a B from you is like an A from anyone else.

HENRY. Well, thank you, Miss Miller.

JUDY. *(Getting up.)* Besides, I don't really believe in grades anymore.

HENRY. Good for you.

JUDY. I think I've grown beyond them.

HENRY. Unfortunately we live in a world which seems to require them. We have to toss them, like bones, to a ravenous administration.

JUDY. Oh God, I know. *They* even wanted me to take an A.

HENRY. And where did they propose you find that A?

JUDY. A professor in Drama saw a rehearsal, and offered to give me a straight A.

HENRY. Ah, but of course that wouldn't count.

JUDY. Oh sure. He said I could register it under Special Topics.

HENRY. Well then, I'm afraid I'd have to go to the Provost. To protest this blatant interference in my course.

JUDY. I just came from the Provost. It was his idea, actually. *(Pause.)*

HENRY. You mean you don't need a grade in my course to graduate.

JUDY. Not any more.

HENRY. You don't really need me at all.

JUDY. Technically, no.

HENRY. Why did you bother to come?

JUDY. I wanted your opinion of my *play!* I wanted to hear what you thought.

HENRY. And I told you: B.

JUDY. Right. Fine. And I'm accepting your B. I'll tell the Registrar. *(She starts out.)*

HENRY. Miss Miller. *(She stops.)* This professor who offered to intrude. Who was he?

JUDY. Who?

HENRY. Do I know him?

JUDY. He's new this year.

HENRY. What's his name?

JUDY. Bob Birnbaum.

HENRY. Bob — ?

JUDY. Birnbaum. *(Pause.)*

HENRY. Of course.

JUDY. What do you mean?

HENRY. Once again Athens is forced to bow to Jerusalem.

JUDY. Explain that, please.

HENRY. I mean the Chosen People always choose to intrude.

JUDY. That's what I thought you meant. *(She strides for the door, then wheels on him.)* All bets are off, Professor Harper. I wouldn't recommend this course to a Nazi! And I'll take a good, solid, Jewish A from Birnbaum! *(She storms out.)*

HENRY. *(Quietly; to himself as he sits.)* Good God. What have I done? *(The lights dim on him as he sits at his desk. Diana crosses the stage hurriedly, carrying a stack of folders. Dave is following her.)*

DAVE. Dean ... ? *(She turns.)* Could I speak to you for a minute, please?

DIANA. I'm sorry, but I'm late for an important meeting.

DAVE. The Committee on Academic Performance, right?

DIANA. That's the one.

DAVE. That's what I've got to speak to you about. *(She stops, looks at him.)*

DIANA. Aren't you that friend of Judy Miller's?

DAVE. David Appleton. My name's coming up before the committee today. I flunked the Chemistry final. I'm not graduating.

DIANA. Chemistry will take care of you. There's infinite salvation: makeup exams, summer school, degrees given out in the fall ...

DAVE. I don't want any of that. I want to switch to your department and be here all next year.

DIANA. Studying what?

DAVE. The Greeks.

DIANA. But we don't have a Classics Department anymore.

DAVE. You have Professor Harper.

DIANA. He may be on sabbatical next year.

DAVE. Oh. Then I'll make up my general requirements till he returns and take Ancient Greek on my own.

DIANA. *(Starting out.)* If you'd make an appointment with Monica, my assistant, we'll discuss all this.

DAVE. No, I've thought it through. I just need your approval.

DIANA. You're talking about another year's tuition.

DAVE. I know. And my dad's cutting me off. But I've gotten a double shift in the cafeteria. I'll get my degree next June, and apply for postgraduate studies with Professor Harper. *(Pause.)*

DIANA. I'll tell the committee you're staying on.

DAVE. Thank you.

DIANA. I envy you.

DAVE. For studying with Harper?

DIANA. For being so sure. *(Judy enters.)*

JUDY. What's going on, Dave?

DAVE. I'm changing my life.

DIANA. Make an appointment if you want to change it back! *(She goes out.)*

JUDY. We have a rehearsal, remember? I'm putting in the final rewrites.

DAVE. Can't make it. Got a class.

JUDY. At this hour? What class?

DAVE. Harper's actually.

JUDY. *Har*per's? *My* Harper?

DAVE. I've been auditing it for the past three weeks.

JUDY. Why?

DAVE. I like him. I like the subject. I like myself when I'm working on it.

JUDY. You never told me that.

DAVE. I knew it would freak you out.

JUDY. Damn right! He's a bigot, Dave.

DAVE. I don't think so.

JUDY. He's an anti-Semite.

DAVE. I don't think so, Judy.

JUDY. I *know* so! *Personally!* He made an anti-Semitic *slur!*

DAVE. He just generalizes, Judy. It's his tragic flaw.

JUDY. I don't buy that, Dave.

DAVE. All right, so he made a crack? So what? People make

ethnic digs all the time in this country. We all get it in the neck —
the Poles, the Italians, now the Wasps.

JUDY. The Jews are different! All though history —

DAVE. So I keep hearing. Still, seems to me you're people, like
everyone else. I think this Jewish thing is getting out of hand. Suddenly nothing counts except you're Jewish!

JUDY. Dave ...

DAVE. No, let me finish, for once in my life! I didn't fall in love
with a Jewish Revolutionary, I fell in love with *you!* I fell in love
with a particular person who liked Springsteen and Moo Sho Pork
and staying in bed all day on Sunday. What happened to all that?
What happens to us next *year?* These are the important things —
not that you're Jewish, for God's sake!

JUDY. I think we're in a little hot water here.

DAVE. I guess we are. *(A bell rings.)* Saved by the bell. *(He
starts off.)*

JUDY. Dave. *(He stops.)* We have rehearsal now.

DAVE. Work around me.

JUDY. It's too late for that.

DAVE. Look, it's his last class. The whole school knows about
this. Everyone wants to see what he's going to say.

JUDY. Not if they're with *Antigone.*

DAVE. Give me an hour.

JUDY. No! It's him or me, Dave. You choose.

DAVE. Be serious.

JUDY. I am. I'll put in Mark Shapiro. I'll replace you. Totally.
(Pause.)

DAVE. Fair enough. *(He starts off again.)*

JUDY. *(Calling after him.)* Then it's true, what my grandmother
said! You people always turn your backs when the chips are down!
(He turns, glares at her, then exits. She speaks softly, to herself.) Oh
Lord. I'm as bad as Harper. *(She goes off slowly the opposite way. The
lights come up on Henry as he comes D., addressing the audience once
again as if it were his class. Dave enters, to sit on the side and listen, as if
he were in class.)*

HENRY. *(To audience.)* This has been a course on tragedy. That is

57

what this course is supposed to be about. *(Pause.)* First, let me remind you what tragedy is *not.* Tragedy has nothing to do with choice. If you can choose, it is not tragic. There are some people who think that our arms race with the Russians is tragic. It is not. It is not, because we have the choice, they have the choice, to say No, to stop, to disarm, to embrace each other in the name of peace at any time. So it is not tragic. It is stupid, yes. It is insane, it is suicidal, it is pathetic, but it is not — repeat Not — tragic, in the true Greek sense of the word. *(Pause.)* Tragedy occurs when you cannot choose, when you have no choice at all. This is hard for Americans to understand. Because most of us are free, or think we are. Nowhere else in the world, and never before in history, have so many people been so free to choose so many destinies. Perhaps, because of this freedom, it is impossible for us to sense what the Greeks called tragedy. We have no oracles, no gods, no real sense of ulitmate authority to insist that if we do one thing, another will inevitably follow. We are free. *(Pause.)* On the other hand, there might come a time to some of us, to one or two, *(He glances at Dave.)* when we get an inkling, a glimmer, a faint shadow of a shadow of what it might have been like for the Greeks when they sat in a theatre and saw the universe close in on a man, or woman, because of some flaw, some excess, some overshooting of the mark ... *(Pause.)* Then the net tightens, and as he struggles, tightens further, until he is crushed by forces total and absurd. *(Pause.)* Then we might be touching the outer borders of tragedy, as the Greeks once knew it. *(Pause. He takes up his book of* Antigone.*)* But I've just discovered something else about tragedy, or at least about Sophoclean tragedy. Something I thought I knew, but didn't understand till now. And that is what the tragic heroes do after the net has closed around them. What they do, even in the teeth of disaster, is accept responsibility, assert their own destiny, and mete out proudly their own punishments. This is what Oedipus does when he puts out his eyes. This is what Antigone does, when she hangs herself. And this is what Creon does, at the end of the same play. He has lost his wife, his children, all he holds dear. And he realizes why: that in his commitment to abstract and dehumanizing laws, he has neglected the very heart of life. And so he banishes himself from his own city. His Polis. He goes. He disappears. He leaves the stage, forever doomed now to wander far from the only community he knows, self-exiled and alone. *(Pause.)* I'll expect all papers under my door by five o'clock this evening. You may retrieve them, graded and with appropriate comments, from the Departmental office next Monday. Enjoy your summer. Read good books. Go to good plays. Think of the Greeks. Thank you and goodbye. *(He sees Dave go, then crosses to his desk, where he leaves his book of* Antigone. *Then he exits, as graduation music comes up loudly: an optimistic piece, played by a brass ensemble. Diana comes out in gown and colorful academic hood. She reads from a formal-looking document.)*

DIANA. Our final award is the Peabody Prize ... *(Reads from card.)* "Offered annually to that student who best combines academic excellence with extracurricular commitment ... " *(To audience.)* It is awarded this year to Judith Rachel Miller, of the graduating class, for her exceptional academic record as well as for her fascinating contemporary version of Sophocles' *Antigone.* *(Applause and cheers. Judy comes on, in academic robes. She accepts an envelope from Diana, who gives her a kiss.)* Congratulations, Judy ... And now refreshments will be —

JUDY. May I say something, please?

DIANA. *(Very reluctantly.)* All right.

JUDY. *(To audience.)* First, I want to thank everyone involved for making our play possible. *(Looks at envelope.)* And I want to thank the Peabody Foundation for making this prize possible. *(Looks out.)* And I want to thank my parents for making *me* possible. *(Diana tries to step in.)* I'm not finished. *(Diana steps back. To audience.)* Lately I've been doing some thinking, and as someone once told me, that's always a good sign. I've been thinking about this prize, for example. I guess it stands for everything I used to believe in: personal ambition ... success ... *(She peeks into the envelope.)* And sure, why not? money ... I mean, these are the things they tell us make our country great ... *(Diana looks worried.)* Trouble is, I'm beginning to think these things aren't so important. Maybe my play hasn't influenced anyone else, but it sure has influenced me. I don't feel good about my life anymore. I don't feel good about my country. I can't accept all this *stuff* that's going on these days. I can't accept it. No, I'm sorry, but I just can't accept it. *(She hands the envelope back to Diana and hurries off.)*

DIANA. Judy! *(She hurries off after Judy, as the lights come up on Henry's office. Dave enters, carrying a note. He finds Henry's book on the desk. He picks it up, looks at it, and starts deciphering the title.)*

DAVE. Alpha... Nu... Tau... Iota... Gamma... Omicron... Nu... Eta ... *Antigone. (Diana enters, no longer in her robes, but still carrying the prize envelope.)*

DIANA. Mr. Appleton? Monica told me you got a note from Professor Harper.

DAVE. *(Indicating the book.)* He said he was leaving me his book.

DIANA. But did he say where he'd *be?* We can't locate him anywhere.

DAVE. He just mentions the book.

DIANA. Oh dear.

DAVE. I'll find him. I'll track him down. Like Telemachus. In the *Odyssey.*

DIANA. You're beginning to sound a little like him.

DAVE. Maybe. In some ways.

DIANA. I suppose you heard about Judy.

DAVE. Saw it. From the sidelines.

DIANA. That girl seems to be interested in systematically hanging herself.

DAVE. She likes to go for broke.

DIANA. This prize is a sizable check. Do you know any cause she'd want to donate it to?

DAVE. Tell you what: I'll ask her. it'll give me an excuse to open diplomatic relations.

DIANA. I have a feeling we may have lost them both forever.

DAVE. Oh God, I hope not.

DIANA. So do I ... Meanwhile, I have no idea how to summarize all this for the Departmental report. What does Sophocles say at the end of that damn play?

60

DAVE. Well, he says that wisdom and reverence lead to happiness ...

DIANA. Oh good. I'll go along with that! Thank you. *(Dave starts out, then stops, turns back.)*

DAVE. But then he goes on to say that we only learn this when we're too old for it to make much difference.

DIANA. Then heaven help us all. *(They look at each other. Blackout.)*

THE END

PROPERTY LIST

ONSTAGE
Desk
2 chairs
Bookcase
Filing cabinet
Hot plate
Coffee pot
2 cracked mugs
Typewritten paper
File of old folders and records
Ashtray
College rule book
Small tape recorder
Sherry
2 murky glasses

OFFSTAGE
Note cards (Diana)
Typewritten script (Dave)
Stack of books (Judy)
Backpack (Judy)
Book (Henry)
Cigarettes (Diana)
Spiral notebook (Judy)
Paperback book (Dave)
Banana (Dave)
Old, worn leather book (Henry)
Envelope (with term paper) (Dave)
Folder (Diana)
Briefcase (with computer printout sheets) (Diana)
Pink slips (Henry)
Stack of folders (Diana)
Formal-looking document (Diana)
Card (Diana)
Envelope (Diana)
Note (Dave)

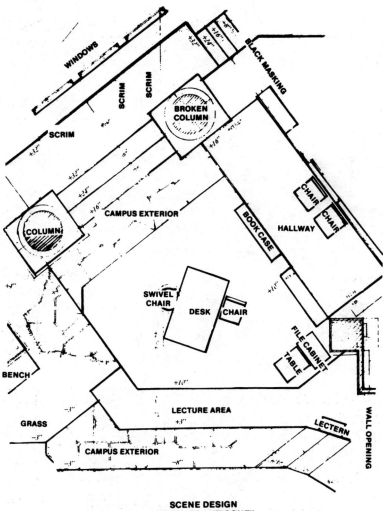

SCENE DESIGN
"ANOTHER ANTIGONE"
(Designed by Steven Rubin for Playwrights Horizons)

NEW
PLAYS

THE AFRICAN COMPANY PRESENTS
RICHARD III
by Carlyle Brown

EDWARD ALBEE'S
FRAGMENTS and THE MARRIAGE PLAY

IMAGINARY LIFE
by Peter Parnell

MIXED EMOTIONS
by Richard Baer

THE SWAN
by Elizabeth Egloff

Write for information as to
availability
DRAMATISTS PLAY SERVICE, Inc.
440 Park Avenue South   New York, N.Y. 10016

NEW
PLAYS

THE LIGHTS
by Howard Korder

THE TRIUMPH OF LOVE
by James Magruder

LATER LIFE
by A.R. Gurney

THE LOMAN FAMILY PICNIC
by Donald Margulies

A PERFECT GANESH
by Terrence McNally

SPAIN
by Romulus Linney

Write for information as to
availability
DRAMATISTS PLAY SERVICE, Inc.
440 Park Avenue South   New York, N.Y. 10016

NEW
PLAYS

LONELY PLANET
by Steven Dietz

THE AMERICA PLAY
by Suzan-Lori Parks

THE FOURTH WALL
by A.R. Gurney

JULIE JOHNSON
by Wendy Hammond

FOUR DOGS AND A BONE
by John Patrick Shanley

DESDEMONA, A PLAY ABOUT A
HANDKERCHIEF
by Paula Vogel

*Write for information as to
availability*
DRAMATISTS PLAY SERVICE, Inc.
440 Park Avenue South   New York, N.Y. 10016